Accidental Vampires
&
The Real Wooden Stake

Book 1: Initiation

Thomas Orr Anderson

Diagrams, cover design, and layout by author

Other books by author:

The Book That Swallows Itself

Master Handbook of Sound Healing

P.S.V.
- Physics of Sound & Vibration for Experiential Practice
expected release: Winter 2019

Published by Swallows Itself Media

ThomasOrrAnderson.com

ISBN: 9781699774564

Dedicated
to
TATA KACHORA

...

around whom

Nature Ever Works

The One True Miracle

...

Teaching Us

The One True Way

.

Where Attention Goes...

Life Flows

•

- Master Kwan

Preliminary Note from Author

It is indeed Wise to admit that...

Since we were Born,

Since we first laughed and cried,

Since first we Breathed the Air of this Earth...

Deep, deep, down...
In our very Core,
In the deepest Center of our Heart...

We have indeed Known the Whole Time,
Without exception, that...

LOVE is the Way.

From Paths Not of LOVE,
This Author does Boldly Say...
We are only as Wise
As we turn away.

Quick Guide
to
Identifying Vampirism

Vampirism is the combination of two essential elements:

Hinting & Blocking

Hinting Draws Attention to Possible States of Affairs...
Both your Attention and the Attention of others.

Hinting arises from two Sources:

Self & Environment

Hinting from Self is... Suspicion.
Hinting from Environment is... Insinuation.

Blocking Prevents Manifestation of Possible States of Affairs...
Those Conceived by both your Self and those Conceived by Others.

Blocking arises from two Sources:

Sphere of Imagination & Surface of Observation

Blocking from Imagination is... Internal Blocking.
Blocking from Surface is... External Blocking.

Where there is both Hinting & Blocking...

There is Vampirism.

Vampirism Calls
for
The Real Wooden Stake.

Quick Guide
to
The Real Wooden Stake

Pay Attention to Attention...
> Both your Attention and the Attention of others.

Understand Futility and Power...
> That which is Futile... does Not and shall Not Manifest;
> That which is Powerful... does and shall Manifest.

Systematically...

Identify Attention in Futility...
> Both your Attention and the Attention of others.

Draw Attention from Futility...
> Both your Attention and the Attention of others.

Cease to Draw Attention into Futility...
> Both your Attention and the Attention of others.

Systematically...

Identify Attention in Power...
> Both your Attention and the Attention of others.

Draw Attention into Power...
> Both your Attention and the Attention of others.

Cease to Draw Attention out of Power...
> Both your Attention and the Attention of others.

Repeat Consistently and Persistently.

Expect Work

In Science, Observing from "the outside,"
So to Speak...
None really Knows what Attention is or how it Works.

On the other hand...
In Direct Experience, Observing from "the inside,"
So to Speak...
One practically Knows what Attention is and how it Works.

In the Domains of our Direct Experience,
Attention Works like a Field...

Illuminating here or there...
Flowing freely or getting stuck.

Attention is Attracted to this or that.
Attention flows to that which Attracts it.

Attention flows within the Spaces of our Direct Experience...
These Spaces are of constantly changing Geometries...
Warped by our Will and...
Made of our Conceptions.

This Work is a Manual for Attention.
This Work is Paying Attention to Attention.

This Work is Work.
Do not expect to find herein anything but Work.
A lazy read... this Work is surely Not.

Yet for One who does the Work...
The Reward is Life.

Two Ways to Read This Work

There are two primary ways to Read this Work.

You, Dear Reader, can
Interpret this Work.

Projecting your own Model
Shall be Called... Interpretation.

You, Dear Reader, can
Understand this Work.

Integrating the Work into your own Model
Shall be Called... Understanding.

To Genuinely Understand this Work
is to
Practice this Work.

What can be Said of this Work
is
Not this Work.

This Work is Not the Words.

The Words are Not this Work.

To Understand is to NOW Do.

To NOW Do is this Work.

Part Zero

Preface

Pay Attention

Most of us were Probably Commanded to do this...
To pay Attention... on countless occasions in childhood...
And throughout our lives...

Sometimes Commanded by Others...
Sometimes by our Selves.

Through Direct Experience and Personal Practice...
And with the help of Feedback from our Environment,
Including from those others who Command us...

We eventually Understand what it means to...

Pay Attention.

Yet this Understanding tends to be partial and inadequate.

We learn to pay Attention to this and to that.
We also learn to ignore some other this and that...
To Not pay those Attention.

Essentially, we learn how to
Do the act of paying Attention....

How to follow the Command...

Pay Attention.

Yet...

Although most of us learn to pay Attention on Command...

Very few of us pay much Attention to Attention itself.

This Work is exactly that.

This is the Work of paying Attention to Attention.

Over the past two decades, I have grown increasingly convinced that the future evolution of Humanity necessarily requires a significantly deepened common Understanding of Attention itself.

Human Knowledge is riddled in countless ways...
Which riddles Obstruct Harmonious Living.

We are plagued by countless unresolved questions...
Questions so deep and far reaching that
Their unresolved nature yields
Immense tragedy and Suffering.

The current human tendency to destroy the very
Environment that sustains us... this tendency is
Directly tied to an array of deep questions about which
There remains perpetual disagreement.

What is Mind?

What is Life?

What is Living and what is Not Living?

What are Beauty and Harmony?

What is Imagination?

What is Self and what is Other?

Who's in charge, if Anyone?

What is Death?

What is Ethical?

Do we have Free Will?

What is Truth?

And so on and so forth...

The great variety of answers to these questions…
Distributed diversely throughout humanity…

These answers tend to compete with one another.

One group believes this and another group believes that.

The beliefs run so deep
and
Yield such tremendous emotive power…
that
One group is actually willing to kill another group…

Simply over their disagreement…
Over and over, throughout history.

Humanity is collectively NOW willing to participate in a
Cooperative effort to destroy the very Life that sustains us.

Humans are collectively NOW willing to participate in
Fundamentally Vampiric systems…

wherein
One trades one's very Life
for the
Minimal rewards
of
Food, Shelter, Sex, Membership, Protection.

By these Vampiric systems,
Vast populations are NOW subjugated
By those who benefit thereby.

The one who has most
is
NOW Vampiring
The one who has least.

Around the deepest of human questions are built...
Countless systems of Vampiric subjugation

and

Countless human Lives are sucked away
by the
Futility required for participation.

By
Agreeing
to...
Subjugate one's Attention to essential Futility,
Vampiric systems provide their subjugated participants with
Minimal rewards.

Humans give away their Attention to such systems
and
Trade their very Life for...

Bread, Houses, Sex, VIP Cards, and Guns.

How are these Vampiric systems maintained?

How do people continue to
NOW have their very Life sucked away
In trade for such minimal rewards?

It is by...
Agreement... Participation... and Lack of Understanding...
that
Vampiric systems are maintained.

Only one who
Agrees to be Vampired... and
Participates in Vampirism... and
Does Not Genuinely Understand...

Only such a one is NOW Vampired.

Conversely... and most importantly... One who...

Does Not Agree to be Vampired...
and
Does Not Participate in the Vampirism...
and who
Genuinely Understands...

Such a person is Not NOW Vampired.

This Work is for those Readers who want both of these:

Not to be Vampired
AND
Not to Vampire.

If you are such a one, Dear Reader,
Then this Work is Probably for you.

If you are Not such a one,
Then beware of your own Reflection,

for...

One who Vampires
is
Vampired Thereby.

Essentially, this Work is born from paying Attention to Attention.

How does Attention Work?

How does Attention flow?

Where is Attention and where does it move?

What makes Attention flow in one direction and Not some other?

How strong is Attention or how weak?

How do the Dynamics of Attention relate to our Life?

How does our Attention relate to feeling more or less Alive?

How does our Attention relate to our Health and lack thereof?

How does our Attention relate to our influence upon others?

How does our Attention relate to others' influence upon our Self?

I have long been devotedly considering these questions and am NOW convinced that their answers comprise a genuine Antidote to the central the problems faced by humanity, both NOW and throughout recorded history.

I am convinced that by collectively Understanding our Attention… we can and will evolve into the Harmony that we all sense as Possible… but which is Not NOW Manifest…

yet…

Will indeed be NOW Manifest.

Here in this Work, I present a simple Model of Attention...

A simple Model that Works.

At first, the Model may seem complex and difficult to
Understand... But once you see the big picture,
Its simplicity and elegance are revealed.

The Model is only complex before you Understand it.
As soon as you Understand the Model, it is simple and easy.

But Not only is the Model simple and easy once you
Understand it,
It is also, more importantly...
Tremendously Useful.

By means of this Model, you can Learn...

Not to be Vampired
AND
Not to Vampire.

Which Requires...

Practice, Practice
AND
More Practice.

Without Practice, Practice, and more Practice...
An intellectual comprehension of this Model is Futile.

Without Practice, Practice, and more Practice...
The very Model itself is Vampiric.

Thus, Dear Reader, be Warned...

Unless you are Willing to actually
Practice Attending your Attention...

Unless you are Willing to Accept
The Responsibility that comes with that Power...

Unless you are Willing to Do the Work...

Continue No Further.

The Sorcerer's foolish Apprentice inevitably suffers
By their lack of Practice, Practice... and more Practice.

To Know and yet Not Do... is Futile.

Before Understanding this Work... that
Futility was Accidental.

Understanding... No more Accident.

This Work is of five primary Parts:

Part 1
Introduction

Part 2
Attention Field Model

Part 3
The Real Wooden Stake

Part 4
Modes of Understanding

Part 5
The Path

How to Read this Work

This Work builds on itself.
That which comes later is incomprehensible
Prior to Understanding what comes before.
Thus, it requires sequential Reading... front to back.

I highly recommend initially Reading the entire Work,

Front to back, somewhat quickly, loosely, softly...
Without putting much effort into Understanding it.

Then, following that quick and easy read,
Begin to Work your way from the beginning...

Taking the time to Follow each step closely...
Perhaps taking notes...
While Not yet expecting to fully Understand.

Then, having made it through those two initial Reads...

First quickly and lightly...
And then more slowly and deeply...

Turn your primary Attention to...

Actually Practicing the Work.

Then, in the midst of your
Consistent Practice,

Read as Helpful.

A Note on Humility

This Work is addressed to you, Dear Reader.

This method of addressing you, Dear Reader, could give the

False impression...

That I, the Author,
Deem myself to be in some higher place...

that
I am the Teacher
and
You, Dear Reader, are the Student.

Thus, it must be Clarified
that

I, the Author,
am also
The Reader to whom this Work is addressed.

As much as
I, the Author, Read this Work...
That much is it also addressed to me.

Both Student and Teacher...
Indeed we are All.

To presume otherwise is Futile.

We are All
In the same Boat...

So to Speak.

A Note on Author's Intention

That this Work is Widely Distributed
and
Commonly Understood...

Such is
The State of Affairs
I
Imagine

.

As much as
This State of Affairs
is made
Manifest...

It is Powerful.

For the Benefit of All Beings...

May It Be So

.

Thomas Orr Anderson
Sewanee, TN
October 11, 2019

Part 1

Introduction

Understanding this Work is both difficult and easy.

It is somewhat like learning a card game such as Poker.

As we are first learning the rules of Poker, those rules may seem somewhat complex and arbitrary... perhaps difficult to understand and remember. But once we are in the flow of the game... once we are really playing... the rules seem simple and somewhat obvious.

At first, Poker may seem difficult.
Once we get the big picture, so to speak...
Poker is quite simple and easy to understand.

This Work is similar in that regard.

At first, this Work may seem difficult, complex, and hard to Understand. But once we get the big picture, it is actually remarkably simple and seems almost obvious.

For this reason... so that you, Dear Reader, may genuinely Understand this Work, it will be useful to prepare accordingly. This Introduction aims to provide you with a big picture view of this Work. Already familiar with that big picture, your Initiation into this Work may be, in the best case, Obvious, simple, and easy.

In order to Accomplish this, in order to provide you with a big picture view of this Work, you will need to be familiar with the Whole Model, in a very general way. This Introduction provides a basic elementary summary of the Model which, in the best case, will make your Reading of this Work obvious, simple, and easy.

The Model includes some basic conceptual elements.
We shall introduce them, one by one...
Hinting at the big picture, Hint by Hint.

Futility

Understanding this Work requires Understanding Futility.

Whenever we pay a great deal of Attention to something...
But that something never, ever, happens...
Such shall be Called... Futile.

Whenever a dream captures all too much of our Attention,
And yet never comes True...
Such shall be Called... Futile.

Whenever someone Hints at a coming prize,
But that prize will, in fact, never Manifest...
Such shall be Called... Futile.

Whenever we put our efforts into domains
Where those efforts remain
Useless and perpetually thwarted,
Such shall be Called... Futile.

And so on...

Power

Understanding this Work also requires Understanding Power.

Power is essentially the opposite of Futility.

Whenever we pay a great deal of Attention to something...
And that something actually happens...
Such shall be Called... Powerful.

Whenever a dream captures much of our Attention
And that dream actually comes True...
Such shall be Called... Powerful.

Whenever someone hints at a coming prize,
And that prize actually Manifests...
Such shall be Called... Powerful.

Whenever we put our efforts into domains
Where those efforts are actually useful
And actually lead to definite intended Results...
Such shall be Called... Powerful.

And so on...

Attention...is Something Like...

A field of Light
That we shine here or there...
On this or that.

Our Attention shines in many sorts of Spaces.

Our Attention shines in Body Space.
We can pay Attention to the feelings in our finger tips or to the feelings in our toes... or both... or neither. Our Attention can shine here and there within the Senses of our Body. At any point in our Body Space, our Attention can be shining brighter, shining more dimly, or hardly shining at all.
Our Attention is like a field of Light within our Body Space.

Our Attention shines in Imagination Space.
We can pay Attention to one idea or to another... or both... or neither. We can pay Attention to one memory or another... or both... or neither. Our Attention can shine here and there within the Space of our Imagination. At any point in our Imagination Space, our Attention can be shining brighter, shining more dimly, or hardly shining at all. Our Attention is like a field of Light within our Imagination Space.

Our Attention also shines in other Dimensions of our experience. As we listen to Music, for example, we can pay more Attention to one instrument or another... or both... or neither. As we smell the world around us, for example, we can pay more Attention to one scent or another... or both ... or neither. In every Dimension of our experience, Attention shines like a field of Light... illuminating this, that, or some other thing... in various degrees of brightness. Our Attention is like a field of Light within every Space of our Direct Experience.

Vampirism

Understanding Vampirism
only
Requires Understanding

Attention... Futility...and Power.

If you, Dear Reader,
NOW Understand these three,

then
You are already prepared to Understand Vampirism,
As that term is used in this Work.

In Direct Experience, Vampirism simply refers to:

Those
Experiences
that
Seem to suck the Life right out of you.

We are all familiar with such experiences.
Vampiric experiences occur in most every domain of Life.

Vampirism can also be described more explicitly...

in a way that is

Not just a story about how it feels to us
Within our Direct Experience.

Vampirism can also be described explicitly...

in a more general way...

A
Way that
Captures its Simple Essence...

The Understanding of which Simple Essence

Yields

Understanding
of its
Unfathomably Complex Manifestations.

This more explicit description
only

Requires an Understanding
of
Attention, Futility, and Power:

Vampirism
is the
Drawing of Attention
Into Futility,
Out of Power.

As much
as
Our Attention is Drawn

Into Futility
and
Out of Power,

That much are we Vampired.

As much
as
Our Attention is Occupied
by...

That
which
Does Not and Shall Not Manifest,

That much are we Vampired.

As our Attention is
Drawn into and occupied by
That which is Futile...

Such an experience

Seems to suck the Life right out of us.

The Antidote for Vampirism

The Antidote for Vampirism is simple.

The Antidote is essentially
to do
the
Opposite of Vampirism.

To remove our Attention from Futility...
To shine our Attention into Power...

Such is the Antidote.

To shine our Attention
within
Our Sphere of Power...

Willing Attention into Life Flow...

Such is the Antidote.

The Antidote for Vampirism shall be Called...

The Real Wooden Stake.

To
Know and to Practice the Antidote
is to be a
Keeper of the Real Woden Stake.

This Work
is
Essentially

The Work
of
Learning,

Practicing,

and when Ready...
Teaching the Antidote.

To
Learn, Practice, and when Ready, Teach

how to
Cease shining our Attention into Futility

and instead
Shine our Attention into Power...

to
Put our Attention where it genuinely Works...

Such is the Work.

To
Genuinely Understand this Work...

is to be
In Possession of the Antidote...

is to be
A Keeper of the Real Wooden Stake.

Probability

Probability plays a central role in this Work.

Most Readers
are
Probably already familiar with Probability.

However,
The Probability of this Work is unusual.

Most of us are familiar
with the
Probability used by Mathematicians and Scientists.

In the domains of Math and Science,

Probability is something we can sometimes calculate
and which can be sometimes
Represented by a number.

Such Probabilities
can sometimes be
Precisely represented by symbols, usually numbers.

For example,
When flipping a simple coin,

The Probability of the coin landing heads-up
is Said to be
50%... or 1/2... or 0.5.

Probabilities of Mathematics and Science tend to be
Precise and represented numerically.

In this Work, Probability is somewhat different.

In this Work...

Probability

is the
Probability of Direct Experience.

Direct Experience
is
Not generally precise

and only very
Rarely can be adequately represented numerically.

The
Probability of Direct Experience

is generally
Vague and relative.

We generally
Cannot assign precise values

to the
Probabilities of Direct Experience.

Let us explore a few examples so as to make this more clear:

Consider...

> *The Probability that...*
> *You will Understand this Work.*
>
> *What do we know about that Probability?*

We can reasonably assume that it is greater than Zero.
We assume that you might Possibly Understand this Work.
We certainly hope so.

Otherwise,
Reading it will be necessarily
Futile and is best avoided.

We can reasonably assume that...

The Probability that you will Understand this Work...
Is greater than Zero.

That assumption is Probably valid.

> *But can we say precisely what that Probability is?*
> *Can we assign a number to that Probability?*
> *Can we calculate that Probability precisely?*

No... we cannot.

The Probability of Direct Experience
is generally
Vague and incalculable.

Let us NOW consider another example:

The Probability that...
You are in fact NOW Reading this sentence.

As you indeed are in fact NOW Reading this sentence...

What is the Probability that...
You are in fact NOW Reading this sentence?

What do we know about that Probability?

As you Read the sentence, we know that it is 100%.

We know that the Probability is One,
As you in fact NOW Read it.

As you are in fact NOW Reading this sentence...

The
Probability

that
You are in fact NOW Reading this sentence

is in fact
Equal to One.

Simple

.

Let us NOW consider another example:

The Probability that...
You will deem this to be a Good Book...

The Probability that you will in fact
Enjoy and appreciate this Work.

What do we Know about that Probability?

We can reasonably assume that it is greater than Zero.

Otherwise
You Probably wouldn't have Read the previous sentences...
or this sentence...
or the sentences that follow.

The Probability that will you enjoy this Work
is
Probably greater than Zero.

If this is your first time Reading this Work,
then you Probably are
Not entirely sure if you will enjoy it.

Thus, the Probability that you will enjoy this Work is Probably less than 100%... less than One. So long as you are Not sure if you will enjoy this Work... then the Probability that you will enjoy it is somewhere between Zero and One.

You may or may Not enjoy this Work. Thus, the Probability of your enjoying this Work is Probably NOW between Zero and One... Greater than 0% and less than 100%.

Let us NOW consider another example:

What is the Probability that...
You NOW Understand this Work?

What do we NOW know about that Probability?

We Know
that the

Probability
that you
NOW Understand this Work

tends to be a
Changing Probability.

Before you Read this Work,
The Probability that you Understood it
was
Probably low... Probably close to Zero.

As you begin to Read this Work,
The Probability that you Understand it
tends to
Increase.

As you continue to Read this Work,
The Probability that you Understand it
tends to
Increase.

That
Probability
tends to
Move

Away from Zero
and
Toward One...

Away from 0%
and
Toward 100%.

On such an occasion that
You Genuinely Understand this Work...

The
Probability
that
You Understand it
will be
NOW One.

We
Imagine
that
This does in fact occur.

Such is the Purpose of this Work.

Let us NOW consider one final example:

What is the Probability that...
You are Not NOW Reading this Work?

What can we Say about that Probability?

So long as
You are

in fact
NOW Reading this Work,

The
Probability
that
You are Not NOW Reading this work
is
NOW equal to Zero.

As you are in fact NOW Reading this Work,
the Probability that you are Not doing so... is 0%.

So long as you are in fact NOW Reading this Work...

We can Say
that
It is Impossible
that
You are Not NOW Reading this Work.

42

Our Model

Having explored a few examples of the Probability of Direct Experience, we are NOW prepared to Consider our Model.

Our Model is comprised of three primary zones:

1. Probability = Zero
2. Probability is greater than Zero and less than One
3. Probability = 1

For any Possible State of Affairs within our Direct Experience, we can often Know in which of these three zones that State of Affairs is located.

If that State of Affairs is Probably Impossible, then that State of Affairs Probably has a Probability equal to Zero.

If that State of Affairs is Probably only Possible, but Not NOW in fact Manifest, then that State of Affairs has a Probability greater than Zero and less than One.

If that State of Affairs is NOW Observed… if it is in fact NOW Manifest… if it is in fact NOW actually happening… that State of Affairs has a Probability equal to One.

Three Zones of Our Model

The first zone, where
Probability equals Zero,
Shall be Called...

Origin.

The second zone, where
Probability is greater than Zero and less than One,
Shall be Called...

Sphere of Imagination.

The third zone, where
Probability equals One,
Shall be Called...

Surface of Observation.

All that takes place
In these three zones,
Shall be Called...

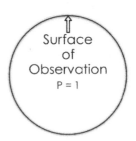

Model.

States of Affairs

One central element of this Work shall be Called...
States of Affairs.

A State of Affairs is simply any thing, situation, concept, idea,
Memory, person, place, pattern, grouping, and so forth.

Essentially, anything that we could give a Name...
We shall Call each such thing... a State of Affairs.

States of Affairs each have Probability.

Our Origin is where Probability equals Zero...
Therefore any State of Affairs with Probably equal to Zero...
Such an Impossible State of Affairs is at

Our Origin... by definition.

Possible States of Affairs that are Not NOW Observed...
Which are only a Possibility but Not NOW Manifest...
Such States of Affairs are within

Our Sphere of Imagination... by definition.

A NOW Observed State of Affairs...
In fact NOW happening in our Direct Experience...
Such a State of Affairs is located on

Our Surface of Observation... by definition.

Conception

Any State of Affairs
NOW in our Model...

Any State of Affairs that
is
In any of our Model's three zones...

Any State of Affairs that we deem to either be...

Impossible... or Possible... or Definite...

Any such State of Affairs shall be Called...

Conceived.

A
Conceived State of Affairs
is a
State of Affairs within our Model.

As a State of Affair enters our Model...

as we deem it to be either...
Impossible... or Possible... or Definite...

Such an entrance into our Model shall be Called...

Conception.

Movement Through Our Model

Every State of Affairs
that
We Conceive

Is NOW

either
At our Origin,
where
Probability equals Zero...

or
Within our Sphere of Imagination,
Where
Probability
is
Greater than Zero and less than One...

or
On our Surface of Observation,
where
Probability equals One.

Yet...
These locations are Not static... they are Dynamical.

Some Possible State of Affairs
may be
More likely NOW than before.

Some Possible State of Affairs
may be
Less likely NOW than before.

As the
Probability of some State of Affairs
is
Conceived to grow…

That
State of Affairs
Moves through our Model,

Toward our Surface of Observation,
Away from our Origin.

Also…

As the
Probability of some State of Affairs
is
Conceived to diminish…

That
State of Affairs
Moves through our Model,

Away from our Surface of Observation,
Toward our Origin.

States of Affairs move through our Model.

Simple Essence of Vampirism

Vampirism

is

Simply

the

Combination

of

Hinting and Blocking.

Hinting

Hinting occurs
as
Our Attention Illuminates some States of Affairs...

Reflections of Attention,
Scattered from those Illuminated States of Affairs...

in turn
Illuminate other States of Affairs.

In other words,

Some States of Affairs,
Attended...

Hint
at
Some other States of Affairs.

Hinting
is the
Scattering of our Attention...
which
Scattered Attention Illuminates elsewhere.

That which
is
Illuminated by the scattered Attention... is Hinted.

That from which the Attention is scattered... Hints.

Hinting, combined with Blocking, is Vampirism.

Blocking

Blocking occurs
as

Some State of Affairs
can...

Neither
Move toward our Surface of Observation...
Toward greater Probability...
Toward Manifestation...

Nor
Move toward our Origin...
Toward lesser Probability...
Toward Impossible.

A
Blocked State of Affairs
is
Stuck in its Probability.

A
Blocked State of Affairs
Flows neither in nor out...
It's Motion is Obstructed
Within our Model.

Blocking is of two forms...
Internal and External.

Internal & External Blocking

Internal Blocking arises from our Sphere of Imagination.
External Blocking arises from our Surface of Observation.

Internal Blocking is mostly Self-made.
Blocking our Self is Said to be... Internal Blocking.

External Blocking, on the other hand, is Not only Self-made.
External Blocking is also Other-made... at least in part.

As States of Affairs in our Environment change...
Such Environmental changes can Block.

Our Environment can change in ways that yield
Blocking within our Model.

Such Blocking can come from
Other people, situations, conditions, systems, groups,
Circumstances, things...
And
Whatever else our Sensors may contact.

Such Blocking from without is Said to be...

External Blocking.

Internal Blocking works in essentially the same way...
But is done unto our Selves.

Hinting & Blocking Yield Futility

As
Some State of Affairs
is
Both
Hinted and Blocked...

That
State of Affairs
is
Made
Futile.

Hinting Draws Attention
to the
State of Affairs.

Blocking Prevents
that
State of Affairs
from
Moving within our Model.

Both
Drawing our Attention
and
Preventing Flow,

Hinting and Blocking
Together are Vampirism.

NOW Prepared for Part 2

Genuinely Understanding the Introduction...
You, Dear Reader, are NOW Prepared for Part 2.

Not Genuinely Understanding the Introduction,
Reading Part 2 may be Futile.

The Introduction has roughly outlined the big picture.
Part 2 fills in some details.

As you proceed, Dear Reader, Remember that...

Until you Genuinely Understand the big picture,
You cannot yet Genuinely Understand the parts.

So...

Be Patient, Sincere, Compassionate... with your Self...

Ever Nurturing that Self-Honesty
Required of every Genuine Student.

Part 2

Attention Field Model

Learning

Learning involves two

Essential complimentary processes.

The first is by way of

New Experiences...

New information, new data.

The second is by way of

Considering familiar experiences

In new ways.

This Work is mostly

of

The Second Way.

Vampirism

This Work isn't really about Vampires....

At least Not the blood-sucking sort.

It's definitely Not about Dracula

Or anything like that.

This Work is about Vampirism,

And most importantly...

This Work is about the Antidote...

The Real Wooden Stake.

So... what is Vampirism?

In this Work,

Vampirism refers to those experiences that...

Seem to suck the Life right out of you.

Vampirism and its Antidote...

This is the Work of Life.

Thus,

Most realistically,

This Work is about Life.

Domains of Vampirism

Vampirism is found
In most every domain of Life.

Experiences with other people
Can be Vampiric.

Experiences with organizations and systems
Can be Vampiric.

Experiences with tasks, roles, and jobs
Can be Vampiric.

Most importantly,

Experiences with our Self
Can be Vampiric.

Essences & Understanding

When something Complex Is Formed

From a Simple Essence,

We can Understand the Complexity

By Understanding the Simple Essence.

Manifestations of Light

Are found throughout the Universe

In Unfathomable Complexity...

But Light has a Simple Essence...

Electromagnetic Waves or Photons.

By Understanding the Simple Essence of Light,

We can Understand its

Unfathomably Complex Manifestations.

Likewise...

By Understanding

The Simple Essence of Vampirism,

We can Understand

Its Unfathomably Complex Manifestations.

Better yet...

By Understanding

The Simple Essence of Life,

We can Understand

Life's Unfathomably Complex Manifestations.

Understanding & Power

By Understanding something,

We are Empowered to

Work with It Effectively.

By Understanding Light,

We are Empowered to

Work with Light Effectively.

By Understanding Vampirism,

We are Empowered

to

Work with Vampirism Effectively.

There are two Ways to
Work with Vampirism Effectively.

The Second Way shall be Called...
The Real Wooden Stake.

This Second Way
is
The Antidote.

Understanding Vampirism
and
Possessing the Antidote
is to
Understand Life.

Understanding Life,
We are Empowered to
Work with Life Effectively.

Reflection & Experience

Our Experience
tends to
Reflect our Intentions.

With Vampiric Intentions,
We are Rewarded with Vampiric Experiences.

If our Intentions are Life-Giving,
We are Rewarded with Life-Giving Experiences.

Dear Reader,
You get what you pay for...
So be careful what you buy.

The Reward of Vampirism is to be Vampired.

The Reward of the Antidote is Life.

Surface of Observation

You, Dear Reader, are an Observer...

One who Observes.

The World around you

Makes Contact with your Sensors...

Essentially, your nerve endings.

You Recognize

The World's Influence

Upon your Sensors.

This shall be Called... Observing.

One who does so
Shall be Called... an Observer.

That Set

of

All the World's Influences upon your Sensors

Shall be Called... your Surface of Observation.

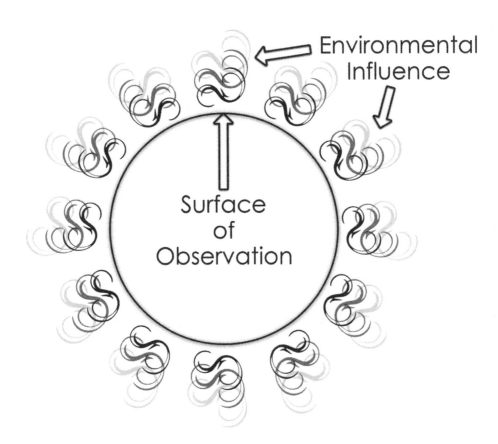

Environmental
Influence

Surface
of
Observation

Probability

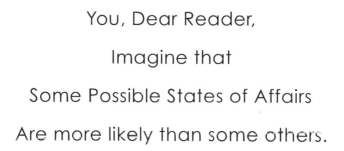

You, Dear Reader,

Imagine that

Some Possible States of Affairs

Are more likely than some others.

You also Imagine that

Some Possible States of Affairs

Are less likely than some others.

How likely you Imagine

Some Possible State of Affairs to Be,

This shall be Called...

The Probability of that State of Affairs.

Range of Probability

Although you, Dear Reader,

Cannot ascribe a precise Value

To the Probability
of
Some Possible State of Affairs...

You can however Know for Certain

That it is somewhere between

Zero and One.

A Probability of Zero means Impossible.

A Probability of One means Definitely.

Every Possible State of Affairs
that
You Imagine

Has a Probability between 0 and 1.

Probability & Surface of Observation

Those States of Affairs NOW Observed...

The Patterns you NOW Sense...

Your Environment's Dynamical Influence

Upon your Sensors NOW...

Has a Probability = 1.

Your Surface of Observation has a Probability = 1.

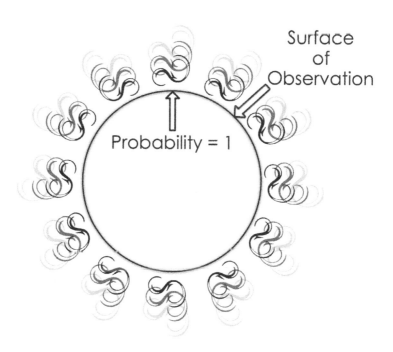

Surface
of
Observation

Probability = 1

Personal Probability

The
Probability of Possible States of Affairs
is
Personal.

That which you NOW Observe
has
Probability = 1

For you... Personally... Dear Reader.

The Probability of that very State of Affairs

May be less than 1, for some other Observer.

The Probabilities in Direct Experience
are
Personal.

Beware of Imagining
that
Other Observers predict like you do.

Each Observer has their own Model.

Sphere of Imagination

Every Possible State of Affairs

That You, Dear Reader,

Imagine of Remember...

If that State of Affairs

Is Not NOW Observed,

Then that State of Affairs

Has Probability less than 1...

For you, Dear Reader.

All those Possible States of Affairs

That you, Dear, Reader,

Imagine or Remember...

That are Not Now Observed...

These constitute a Set.

That Set shall be Called your...

Sphere of Imagination.

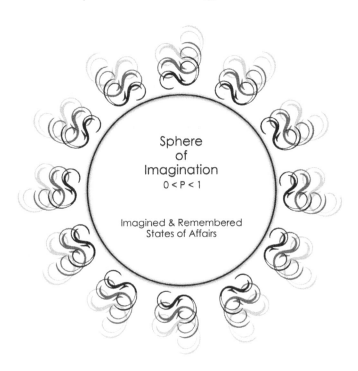

Sphere
of
Imagination
$0 < P < 1$

Imagined & Remembered
States of Affairs

Origin

We Call

That region where Probability = 1...

Your Surface of Observation.

We Call

That region where Probability is less than 1...

Your Sphere of Imagination.

We Call

That point where Probability = 0...

Your Origin.

Model

We NOW have a Model.

That Sphere Defined by...

Your Origin...
&
Your Surface of Observation...
&
Your Sphere of Imagination...

Shall be Called...

Your Model.

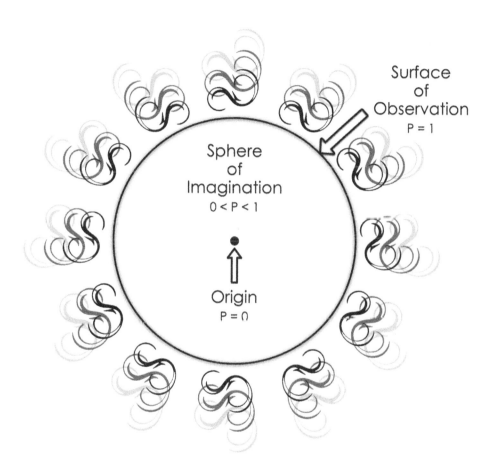

Surface
of
Observation
$P = 1$

Sphere
of
Imagination
$0 < P < 1$

Origin
$P = 0$

For you, Dear Reader,

We shall Call this… your Model.

Reading

You, Dear Reader,

Recognize Patterns
in your
Surface of Observation.

You also Recognize Patterns
in your
Sphere of Imagination.

Your
Acts of Pattern Recognition
Shall be Called... Reading.

Recognizing Patterns
in your
Senses...
you are
Reading your Surface of Observation.

Recognizing Patterns
in your
Imagination and Memories...
you are
Reading your Sphere of Imagination.

Limited Reading Capacity

You, Dear Reader,

Cannot Read Everything at Once.

You can only simultaneously Read
Subsets of Your Model....

Subsets
of
Your Surface of Observation
&
Your Sphere of Imagination.

You, Dear Reader,

Have a Limited Reading Capacity.

What are you Reading NOW?

Attention

You, Dear Reader,

Are NOW Reading

Subsets of your Model.

The Set of all those
Subsets You NOW Read

Shall be Called...

Your Attention.

Your Attention

is

That Which You Are NOW Reading.

Spacetime

The word
"Space"

usually refers to that

Three-Dimensional Space
that we can
Measure as Distance...

in
meters, feet, inches, miles, and so forth.

Further,
we conceive a

Fourth Dimension
we
Measure as Time...

in
seconds, millennia, days, or tiks of a Clock.

This Spacetime
has
Four Degrees of Freedom...

In that you can
Designate or Identify

Any location,
By your Rulers...

At any Time,
By your Clock.

Designating Relations to your Chosen Origin,

Length, Width, Height, & Time

can

Identify
any
Conceived Spacetime Event
in the
World around you.

Dimensions

The Four Degrees of Freedom of Spacetime...

Length, Width, Height, & Time...

We Call these... Four Dimensions.

Thus, we Call Spacetime... Four-Dimensional.

Yet...

Not all Degrees of Freedom are
Length, Width, Height, or Time.

Colors change,
Smells change,
Feelings change,
Volume changes,
Freshness changes,
Honesty changes,
Creativity changes...

Any conceived Direction of Change

Shall be Called... a Dimension.

HyperSpace

We Imagine Spaces
with
As many Dimensions as we Conceive...
Not Limited to the Four Dimensions of Spacetime.

Any Conceivable Direction of Change

Can be Conceived as a Dimension.

Any Conceivable Set of Dimensions

Can be Conceived as a Space.

A
Conceived Space
of
More than Four Dimensions

Shall be Called a...

HyperSpace.

Your Model is a HyperSpace

Your Model Includes

both

That Which Is NOW Observed
and
That Which is NOW Imagined or Remembered.

As you Recognize

Patterns in your Model...

As you Recognize

Patterns in your Surface of Observation
and
Patterns in your Sphere of Imagination...

You Conceive Directions of Change.

All those Ways
that you
Conceive States of Affairs

to
Change... or Possibly Change...

Those Ways
are the
Degrees of Freedom of your Model.

Your Model
is a
HyperSpace of that many Dimensions.

As many Directions of Change
That you Conceive...

Your Model
is a
HyperSpace of that many Dimensions.

States of Affairs

You, Dear Reader,

Conceive
some
Imagined State of Affairs

to be
More likely
than
Some other Imagined State of Affairs.

The
More likely
You Imagine some State of Affairs to be,

the
Closer
That State of Affairs
is to your
Surface of Observation...

The closer its Probability is to One.

The
Less likely
You Imagine some State of Affairs to be,

The
Closer
That State of Affairs is to your Origin...

The closer its Probability is to Zero.

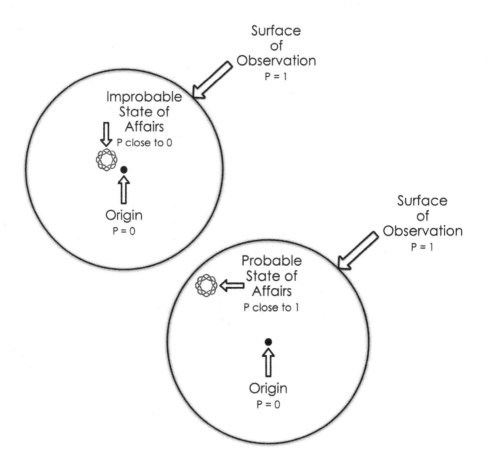

Surface
of
Observation
P = 1

Improbable
State of
Affairs
P close to 0

Origin
P = 0

Surface
of
Observation
P = 1

Probable
State of
Affairs
P close to 1

Origin
P = 0

Warping

Some Possible State of Affairs
Imagined by you, Dear Reader,

can become
More likely than before...

or
can become
Less likely than before.

As
Some Imagined State of Affairs

becomes
More or less likely than before...

As its Probability
either
Increases or Decreases,

That Change shall be Called...

Warping.

Manifestation

Some Possible State of Affairs...
Imagined by you, Dear Reader,

Can Become
Observed.

The Probability of some State of Affairs
Imagined by you, Dear Reader,
Can Become One.

Transitions

from
Your Sphere of Imagination,
where
Probability is less than One,

to
Your Surface of Observation,
Where Probability is One...

Such Transitions shall be Called...

Manifestation.

Manifestation
From P < 1 to P = 1

What was Possible NOW Is.

Futility

As some State of Affairs,

Imagined by you, Dear Reader,

Remains

Necessarily within the Sphere of Imagination...

Necessarily Unmanifest...

Necessarily of Probability less than One...

Such a State of Affairs shall be Called...

Futile.

That which is Futile does Not Manifest.

Power

As some State of Affairs,
Imagined by you, Dear Reader,
Manifests...

As the
Probability of some Imagined State of Affairs...

Changes
from
less than One
to
One...

As some State of Affairs is NOW Observed,
Having before been only Imagined...

Such a State of Affairs shall be Called...

Powerful.

That which is Powerful Manifests.

Attention in Manifestation

As some State of Affairs,
Imagined by you, Dear Reader,

Manifests,

That State of Affairs is Powerful.

If that State of Affairs Is
Within your Attention...

If that State of Affairs
Is Being NOW Read...

Then that State of Affairs
is
More Powerful
than
If Not Being NOW Read.

Attention yields Power to Power.

Attention Field

Your Attention, Dear Reader,
Is a Field within your Model.

At any location within your Model,

Your Attention Field
has
Strength or Magnitude.

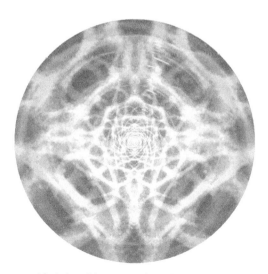

Light = Strong Attention Field
Dark = Weak Attention Field

Imagine...

within
The HyperSpace of your Model...

A Field of Light.

Where you are NOW Reading,
There is Light.

Where you are Not NOW Reading,
There is Not Light.

Illuminating
Some regions of your Model
More than others...
Some less than others...

This Dynamical Field of Illumination...

NOW Here, NOW There...
within your
Sphere of Imagination
and
Surface of Observation...

Shall be Called...

Your Attention Field.

Minimal Attention Field

Where there is No Attention...

In those regions of your Model
Not NOW Read...

Attention Field Strength equals Zero.

Zero is the Minimum Attention Field Strength.

Where Attention Field Strength is Zero...

Where Attention Field Strength is at its Minimum...

You are Not NOW Reading.

Maximal Attention Field

Minimum Attention Field Strength
is
Simple to Conceive...

It is simply equal to Zero
Where you are Not NOW Reading.

Maximum Attention Field Strength
is
More complex to Conceive.

To make it easier, we shall Conceive...

Total Attention Field Strength
as
Equal to One.

Thus,
Maximum Attention Field Strength equals One.

In such a case that
Attention is NOW Reading
Only One State of Affairs...

Attention Field Strength equals One
For that State of Affairs.

Attention Field Dynamics

In any region of your Model, Dear Reader,

Your Attention Field Strength
Fluctuates...
Increases and Decreases.

Fluctuating,
It shall be called... Dynamical.

Thus, your Attention, Dear Reader,
Is a Dynamical Field.

Fluctuations
In the Dynamical Field
That is your Attention...

These shall be Called...

Your Attention Field Dynamics.

Model Structures

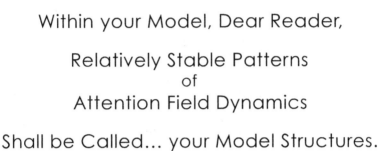

Within your Model, Dear Reader,

Relatively Stable Patterns
of
Attention Field Dynamics

Shall be Called... your Model Structures.

Imagine your Model to be
A Body of Water...

And your Model Structures to be
Whirlpools in that Water.

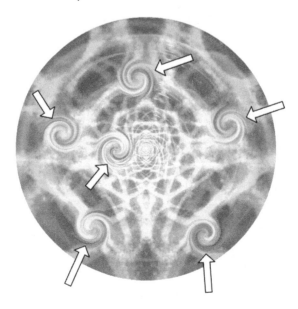

Mass of Model Structures

As your
Model Structures, Dear Reader,

Increase in these two ways…

Attention Field Strength
&
Duration…

Those Model Structures are Said to…

Grow more Massive.

Duration
and
Attention Field Strength

Yield Mass
within
Your Model.

Gravity in Model

In the HyperSpace of your Model, Dear Reader,

Attention
is
Attracted to Mass.

Your Attention
is
Attracted
to...

Those regions of your Model where

Relatively stable Patterns
of
High Attention Field Strength
Yield Mass.

That which you have Attended much
Attracts your Attention, Dear Reader.

Futile Mass

Within your Model, Dear Reader,

Necessarily Unmanifest Mass

Shall be Called...

Futile Mass.

Futile Mass

is

That Mass which does Not Manifest.

Two Forms of Futile Mass

Futile Mass is of two primary Forms.

The first Form
is
That which cannot Manifest.

The first Form
is
Prevented by the Way of Things.

The second Form
is
That which can Manifest, yet does Not.

The second Form
is
Not Prevented by the Way of Things.

The second Form
is
Possible, and yet Not.

Futile Mass is Vampiric

As your Attention, Dear Reader,
Is Attracted to Futile Mass...

The Strength of Attraction

Increases as Futile Mass increases
and
Decreases as Futile Mass decreases.

That Attraction of your Attention to Futile Mass
Shall be Called... Vampiric.

Your Experience
of that
Futile Attraction, Dear Reader,
is an
Experience of Vampirism.

Where Does the Life Go?

In Vampiric Experiences...

That seem to suck the Life right out of you...

Where does the Life go?

NOW we Know.

It goes to Futile Mass.

It goes to

Relatively stable Futile Structures
Within your Model, Dear Reader...

To those Imagined States of Affairs
Which never Manifest...

But which Attract your Attention.

Attention & Life

You have Learned, Dear Reader,
that
Futile Mass...

Relatively Stable Structures within you Model
that
Remain Unmanifest...

Provided Attention Strength and Duration,

Such Structures grow more Massive...

Attracting Allention ever-more thereto.

As your
Attention is Attracted to Futile Mass,

it
Seems
like the
Life is being sucked right out of you.

Outflow

As some State of Affairs,

Imagined by you, Dear Reader,

Transitions toward your Surface of Observation...

As you
Imagine
that
State of Affairs
to be
More Probable...

That Outward Current shall be Called...

Your Outflow.

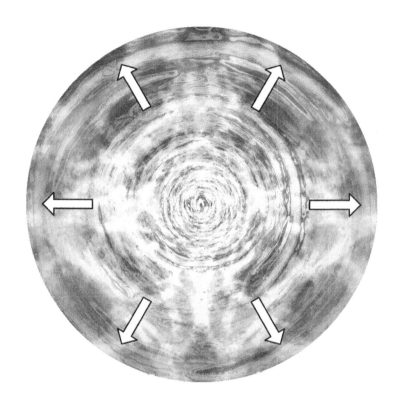

Within your Model, Dear Reader,

Outflow is that Current

Away from your Origin...

Toward your Surface of Observation.

Inflow

As some State of Affairs,

Imagined by you, Dear Reader,

Transitions toward your Origin...

As you
Imagine
that
State of Affairs
to be
Less Probable...

That Inward Current shall be Called...

Your Inflow.

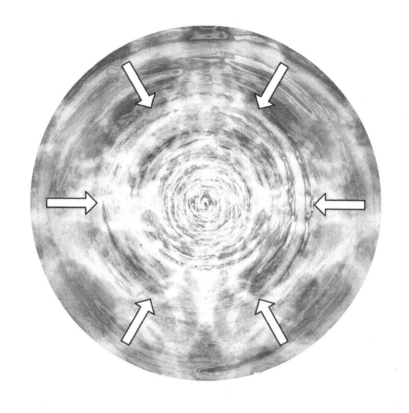

Within your Model, Dear Reader,

Inflow is that Current

Away from your Surface of Observation

Toward your Origin.

Attention Field Grows

As your Attention, Dear Reader,
Freely follows the Life Flow,

BOTH
Outflow from your Origin
Toward your Surface of Observation...

AND
Inflow toward your Origin
From your Surface of Observation...

Your total Attention Field Strength
Grows.

Even as it Grows,

We shall Call...
The Total Attention Field Strength...
One.

Thus, as your

As your Total Attention Field Strength Grows,
One Grows.

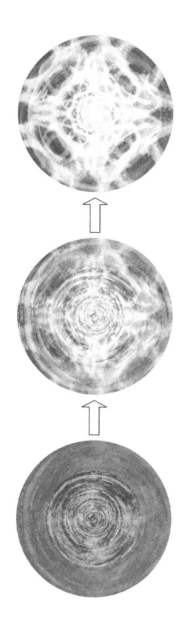

Attention Field Strength Grows

Attention Field Diminishes

As your Attention, Dear Reader,
Follows Not the Life Flow,

Neither as Outflow from your Origin
Toward your Surface of Observation...

Nor as Inflow toward your Origin
From your Surface of Observation...

Your total Attention Field Strength
Diminishes.

Even as it Diminishes,

We shall Call...
The Total Attention Field Strength...
One.

Thus, as your
Total Attention Field Strength Diminishes,

One Diminishes.

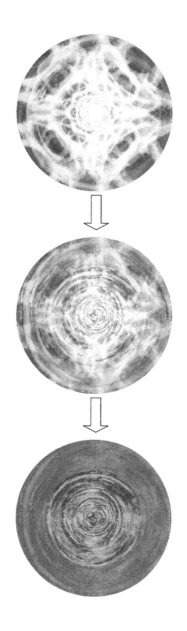

Attention Field Strength Diminishes

Attention Path Guidance

As your Attention Field, Dear Reader,
Dynamically Flows within your Model...

Illuminating some States of Affairs, then others...

within

Your Sphere of Imagination
and on
Your Surface of Observation...

The Paths of Change
are
Guided in two ways:

Attraction to Mass

and

Warping.

Passive Attention Guidance

The first way

Attention Paths are Guided

Is Said to be... Passive.

Attention simply Flows

Toward Mass

To which it is Attracted...

Much like Newton's Gravitational Force

Pulling an Apple

Toward the Earth.

Active Attention Guidance

The second way

Attention Paths are Guided

Is Said to be... Active.

The Paths of Attention Flow

Are Altered by

The Very Space in which Attention Flows.

Much like Einstein's General Relativity,

Guiding an apple

Toward the Earth...

By Warping the Space in which it moves.

Simple Essence of Action

Just as the
Unfathomably Complex Manifestations of Light
can be Understood by
Understanding the Simple Essence of Light...

Electromagnetic Waves or Photons...

Just as the
Unfathomably Complex Manifestations of Life
can be Understood by
Understanding the Simple Essence of Life...

Life Flow...

Likewise, the
Unfathomably Complex Manifestations of Action
can be Understood by
Understanding the Simple Essence of Action...

Will.

The Simple Essence of Action shall be Called...

Will.

Will is Warping

To Will is to Warp.

As you, Dear Reader,

Warp the Space of your Model...

This is Said to be... Willing.

This, Dear Reader,

is

The Simple Essence of your Action.

Will Guides Attention

The Flow of your Attention, Dear Reader,
is
Guided by the Attraction of Mass.

This is Passive.

The Flow of your Attention
is also
Guided by Warping of your Model.

This is Active.

Warping of your Model is Will.

Warping is Active.

Your Will is Active.

Recognizing Will

How do you, Dear Reader,
Recognize that which you are NOW Willing
?

How do you know which way
You are Guiding Attention Flow
?

This is done

by

Self-Reflection.

Attention on Attention

Shall be Called... Self-Reflection.

Self-Reflection

Your Attention, Dear Reader,
Illuminates its own Reflection.

The Flow of your Attention
is
Reflected in
All that you NOW Attend.

Those Patterns NOW Read
In your Model...

Those Patterns NOW Illuminated
by
The Light of your Attention...

In those Attended Patterns is NOW
The Reflection of your Attention.

Attending Reflection of Attention
shall be Called...

Self-Reflection.

Hinting

As the Light of your Attention, Dear Reader,

Illuminates some Pattern in your Model...

Attends some Possible State of Affairs...

That Attended Pattern
Radiates into your Model.

By that Radiation,
Other Patterns are Illuminated.

Other Possible States of Affairs are Attended
by the
Scattered Radiant Illumination.

This Process, wherein

Some Attended Pattern,
Some Attended State of Affairs,

Radiates Scattered Attention...

Illuminating other Possible States of Affairs...

Your Attention Flowing thereto...

This shall be Called...

Hinting.

Two Forms of Hinting

There are two Forms of Hinting.

The first Form Radiates
From Imagined States of Affairs.

The second Form Radiates
From Observed States of Affairs.

The first Form shall be Called...
Suspicion.

The second Form shall be Called...
Insinuation.

These Forms are
Identified by their Source...

Surface of Observation
or
Sphere of Imagination.

Suspicion

When a Hint Radiates
From your Sphere of Imagination,
That Hint is Said to be... Suspicion.

As the Light of your Attention, Dear Reader,
Illuminates some Imagined State of Affairs...

Attention Field Fluctuations, Radiating therefrom,

Illuminate other Imagined States of Affairs.

Those States of Affairs,

Illuminated by that Scattered Radiation,

Are Said to be... Suspected.

Suspecting is Suspicion.

Insinuation

When a Hint Radiates
From your Surface of Observation,
That Hint is Said to be... Insinuation.

As the Light of your Attention, Dear Reader,
Illuminates some Observed State of Affairs...

Attention Field Fluctuations, Radiating therefrom,

Illuminate some Imagined States of Affairs.

Those States of Affairs,

Illuminated by that Scattered Radiation,

Are Said to be... Insinuated.

Insinuating is Insinuation.

Blocking

It is Blocking that makes a Hint Vampiric.

When some State of Affairs is Obstructed...

When some State of Affairs enters Not Life Flow...

When Some State of Affairs moves Not...

Neither toward your Surface of Observation...

Nor toward your Origin...

Such a State of Affairs is Said to be...

Blocked.

That which Blocks a State of Affairs is Said to be...

Blocking.

Internal Blocking

As your Sphere of Imagination is Warped

Such that some State of Affairs is Blocked...

Such is Said to be Internal Blocking.

Internal Blocking is Self-made.

Internal Blocking is done unto your Self.

By Warping you Sphere of Imagination,

You Block...
as
Your Warping prevents Life Flow
For some Imagined State of Affairs.

Blocked,
That Imagined State of Affairs moves
Neither inward nor outward
Within your Model.

External Blocking

As your Sphere of Observation is Warped

Such that some State of Affairs is Blocked...

Such is Said to be External Blocking.

External Blocking can be Other-made...
Partially.

External Blocking can be done unto you.

By changing Environmental conditions,

Your Environment Blocks...

In such cases that
Environmental changes prevent Life Flow
For some Imagined State of Affairs.

Blocked,
That Imagined State of Affairs moves
Neither inward nor outward
Within your Model.

Hinting & Blocking are Vampiric

The combination
of
Hinting and Blocking
Yield Futility.

Hinting and Blocking Together
are
Vampiric.

That State of Affairs
which is
Both Hinted and Blocked...

Such a State of Affairs
is
Futile.

As Hinting and Blocking
Work together...

There is Futility...
There is Vampirism.

Vampirism Calls
for
The Real Wooden Stake.

Part Three

The Real Wooden Stake

NOW Ready

If you, Dear Reader,
Do Not Genuinely Understand Parts 1 & 2,

Reading Part 3 is Futile...

You are Not NOW Ready
for
The Real Wooden Stake.

If you, Dear Reader,
Genuinely Understand Parts 1 & 2,

Reading Part 3 is Powerful...

You are NOW Ready
for
The Real Wooden Stake.

Healing & Vampiring

Understanding the Model
is
Power.

Power can be Used
in
Two Ways.

Power can be Used
for
Healing.

Power can be Used
for
Vampiring.

Healing

By Self-Reflection,

Your Attention, Dear Reader,

Can Recognize its own Flow.

By Will, your Model is Warped.

As you, Dear Reader,

Warp your Model

such that

Attention joins the Current of Life Flow...

This shall be Called...

Healing.

Vampiring

By Self-Reflection,

Your Attention, Dear Reader,

Can Recognize its own Flow.

By Will, your Model is Warped.

As you, Dear Reader,
Warp your Model

such that

Attention leaves the Current of Life Flow...

This shall be Called...

Vampiring.

Two Ends of the Stake

The Antidote to Vampirism...

The Real Wooden Stake
has
Two Ends.

Without both Ends,
There is no Antidote.

With both Ends,
The is NOW Antidote.

The first End
is
Toward Healing.

The second End
is
Away from Vampirism.

Both Ends are the Antidote;

One End is Not the Antidote.

Healing: The First End

The first End of the Real Wooden Stake
is
Toward Healing.

By Self-Reflection,
Your Attention, Dear Reader,
Recognizes its own Flow.

As your Attention Recognizes its own Flow,

Warping your Model
such that
Attention Flow joins Life Flow...

You, Dear Reader, are Said to be...

Healing.

This is the first End.

Unvampiring: The Second End

The second End of the Real Wooden Stake
is
Away from Vampiring.

As your Attention, Dear Reader,
By Self-Reflection,
Recognizes its own Flow,

Warping your Model
such that
Attention Flow ceases to leave Life Flow...

You, Dear Reader, are Said to be...

Unvampiring.

This is the second End.

Keeper of the Stake

Joining the Life Flow,
Ceasing to leave Life Flow,

These two together are...

The Antidote...
The Real Wooden Stake.

If you, Dear Reader,
Genuinely Understand
The Work thus far...

You are NOW Said to be...
Possessing the Antidote.

You are NOW

A Keeper of the Real Wooden Stake.

Part Four

Modes of Understanding

Simple Spectator

As you, Dear Reader,
First Open your Eyes...

Simply Observe
the
Unfathomably Complex Manifestations of Light...

You are a Simple Spectator of Light.

As you, Dear Reader,
First Open your Attention...

Simply Observe
the
Unfathomably Complex Manifestations of Life...

You are a Simple Spectator of Life.

Informed Spectator

As you, Dear Reader,
Begin to Understand

The Simple Essence of Light,

You become an Informed Spectator of Light.

As you, Dear Reader,
Begin to Understand

The Simple Essence of Life,

You become an Informed Spectator of Life.

Beginning Student

As you, Dear Reader...

Understanding
the
Simple Essence of Light,

Also begin to Understand
the
Unfathomably Complex Manifestations of Light,

You are a Beginning Student of Light.

As you, Dear Reader,

Understanding
the
Simple Essence of Life,

Also begin to Understand
the
Unfathomably Complex Manifestations of Life,

You are a Beginning Student of Life.

Practicing Student

As you, Dear Reader...

Understanding

the

Simple Essence

as well as the
Unfathomably Complex Manifestations

of
Light...

Warp your Spacetime

by

Will...

You are a Practicing Student of Light.

As you, Dear Reader...

Understanding

the

Simple Essence

as well as the
Unfathomably Complex Manifestations

of
Life...

Warp your Model

by

Will...

You are a Practicing Student of Life.

Initiate

As you, Dear Reader,

Will Warping of Spacetime,

To Both Heal and Unvampire,

You are an Initiate of Light.

As you, Dear Reader,

Will Warping of your Model,

To Both Heal and Unvampire,

You are an Initiate of Life.

Polar Initiate

As you, Dear Reader,

Use your Willed Warping
to
Either Heal or Unvampire,

But Not both...

You do Not NOW Possess the Antidote.

You are Not NOW
A Keeper of the Real Wooden Stake.

You are Said to be a... Polar Initiate.

Possessing only one End
is
To Possess no Stake.

Polar Initiates Require Partners

If you, Dear Reader,
are a
Polar Initiate,

You can Possess the Stake
in
Partnership with another Polar Initiate.

You Possess only one End,
Which is Possessing no Stake.

Another Polar Initiate
Possesses only the other End,
Which also is no Stake.

In Partnership,
You and the other Polar Initiate
No longer Possess no Stake.

In Partnership,
You comprise a Keeper of the Stake.

Together,
You Possess the Antidote.

Practice

Your Attention, Dear Reader,
Is Not NOW Sufficient
To Read your Whole Model.

You NOW Read
Only some Subset of your Model.

Thus,
Genuine Understanding Requires Practice.

Practice
is
Using Will to Warp your Model...

such that

The Flow of Attention

Becomes

Life Flow Itself.

The Warning

Within your Imagination, Dear Reader,

Are some Possible States of Affairs

wherein

You Use your Will
as
The AntiStake.

You Accidentally Imagine...

UnHealing and Vampiring...

Guiding Attention into Futility...

Out of Life Flow.

Within your Imagination, Dear Reader,

You Accidentally Imagine

Making Poison rather than the Antidote.

Thus, the Warning is Simple:

You, Dear Reader,

are

Always and without exception,

The Recipient of your own Reflection.

What you Make...
You Take.

False Teacher

Prior to Initiation...

Prior to Possessing the Antidote...

Prior to being
a
Keeper of the Real Wooden Stake...

You, Dear Reader,

Accidentally Imagine
Possessing the Antidote NOW.

You, Dear Reader,

Accidentally Imagine
Being NOW a Keeper of the Real Wooden Stake.

Such a one shall be Called...

Accidental False Teacher.

False Teacher Returns to Origin

Initiated,

You, Dear Reader,

Cannot be a False Teacher.

Being a False Teacher
is
To Not be Initiated.

Initiated,

You, Dear Reader,

Cannot be a False Teacher.

False Teacher
Returning to your Origin

Shall be Called...

Initiation.

Your Origin is Impossible.

Initiated,

Your Origin
is
False Teacher's Home.

Pre-Teacher - Post-Initiation

Initiated, you, Dear Reader,
are
NOW
A Keeper of the Real Wooden Stake.

Not being such a One
is to
Not NOW be Initiated.

Initiated,

False Teacher is NOW Returned to your Origin…

False Teacher is NOW Impossible.

Thus, you, Dear Reader,

Initiated…
Cannot be a False Teacher.

Real Teacher

Initiated...

Genuinely Understanding

that you are

Not NOW Prepared
to be
A Real Teacher...

Your Model

is, by that Understanding,

Somewhat Transparent to the Universe.

Being somewhat Transparent,

That-Which Flows-Through-You-Unobstructed

is
The Real Teacher.

Wisdom

NOW Initiated...
NOW a Keeper of the Real Wooden Stake...

NOW Genuinely Understanding
That you are Not NOW Prepared
to
Be a Real Teacher.

NOW having Grown somewhat Transparent...

Some of the Universe's Fluctuations
NOW Flowing through you Unobstructed...

You, Dear Reader, can NOW Recognize
The Patterns of your very Transparency.

You Recognize
Where Light NOW Flows Unobstructed...
and
Where Light NOW Flows Not.

Recognizing such shall be Called...

Wisdom.

Part Five

The Path

The Path

Your Path, Dear Reader,
is
Composed of One Simple Essence.

Though a Simple Essence,
it is yet
One of many Faces.

Your Path, Dear Reader,

Is Said to be...
The Reading of those Faces.

Those Faces are your Path.

Thus, it may be Said that...
Your Path is Reading your Path.

Discovering your Path,
Dear Reader,
Is to be on It.

Practice

One Face of your Path, Dear Reader,
Shall be Called...

Practice.

To Truly Know this Face
is to
Know Them All.

All Faces of your Path
are...

In Practice...
Of Practice...
For Practice...

About... Because of... From... To...

Practice

∞

.

Domains of Practice

Your Model, Dear Reader,
is
Composed of Three Primary Domains:

Origin

Probability = Zero

Surface of Observation

Probability = One

Sphere of Imagination

Zero < Probability < One

Origin: Sink & Source

Your Origin, Dear Reader, serves

Two Primary Roles in your Practice.

Your Origin serves as

A Sink.

By your Will,
You, Dear Reader,

Divert the Paths of Futile Mass
Toward your Origin.

This is an Active Role.

This uses your Will.

Your Origin also serves as

A Source.

From your Impossible Origin,

Possible States of Affairs...
Patterns in your Model...

Radiate.

This is a Passive Role.

Your Origin...

Being Impossible...

is
Impossible to Attention and Will.

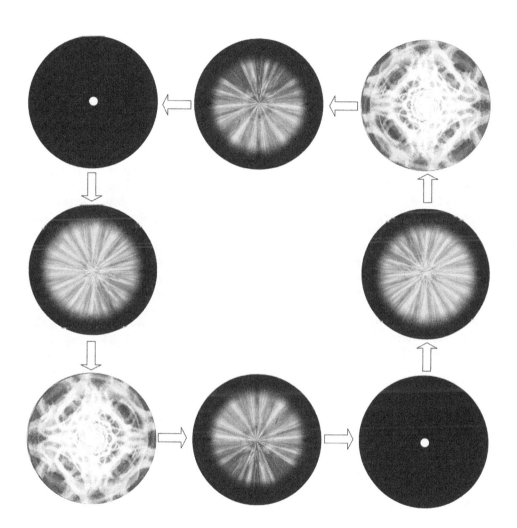

Origin as Sink

Your Attention, Dear Reader,

Illuminates
Futile Mass within your Model.

Illuminated,
Futile Mass is Recognized.

Your Will, Dear Reader,

Warps your Model Dimensions

so as to

Move Futile Mass
Toward your Origin.

You, Dear Reader,

By Will
Bend your Model

so as to

Form Funnels to your Sink...
Funnels to your Origin...

where

Futile Mass is Recycled.

Using Will,

This is an Active Role.

Origin as Source

Your Attention Field, Dear Reader,

Cannot Penetrate the Impossible.

Your Attention Field
Reaches Not your Origin.

Rather,
Your Attention, Dear Reader,

Radiates therefrom.

The Radiation of your Attention

From your Origin
Occurs without Will.

Relative to your Will, Dear Reader,

Radiation of Attention from your Source
is a
Passive Role.

However...

Although

Your Attention cannot Penetrate your Origin...

Your Attention can Surround your Origin.

You, Dear Reader, can Attend

The Radiant Attention Field at your Origin.

To Attend your Source Radiation
is an
Active Role.

By your Will, Dear Reader,

You Warp your Model

So as to Surround your Origin with Attention...

Attending the Field Radiant therefrom.

Origin & Little Death

As your Attention, Dear Reader,

Surrounds your Origin...
Attention Field Strength Condensing
Around that Impossible Point...

There exists a Threshold.

The Attention Field Density
Having Attained this Threshold...

Mutual Attraction within that Dense Field
Transitions to Infinity...
Transitions to Impossible...

Your Whole Attention Field
has
Returned to your Origin...

Where it is NOT.

This shall be Called...

Your Little Death.

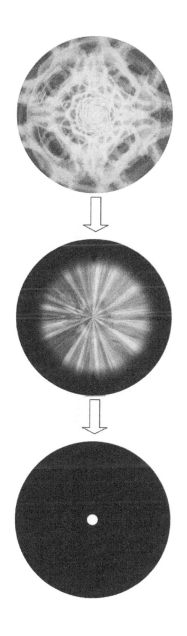

Attention Returns to Origin

Origin & Rebirth

In your Little Death, Dear Reader,

Your Whole Attention Field
has
Ceased to be.

In such a case, Dear Reader,
You are NOT.

Having been NOT...

Your Attention Field
Re-Radiates from your Origin...

You, Dear Reader,
NOW Are Having NOT Been.

Such a case shall be Called...

Your Rebirth.

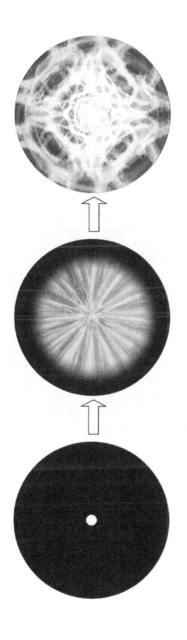

Attention Returns from Origin

Surface of Observation in Practice

Your Surface of Observation, Dear Reader,
is the
Interface

where

Your Environment
meets
Your Model.

Your Sensations
are
Patterns on that Surface.

Your Behaviors
are also
Patterns on that Surface.

Both
Your Senses and your Behaviors
are
Patterns on your Surface of Observation.

Two Forms of Sensations in Practice

Your Sensations, Dear Reader,

are of

Two Primary Forms...

Self and Other.

On your Surface of Observation,

are

States of Sensation Affairs
Conceived to be Self

and

States of Sensation Affairs
Conceived to be Other.

Surface of Sensed Self

Between

Imagined and Observed
States of Sensation Affairs
That you, Dear Reader,
Conceive to be Self...

and

Imagined and Observed
States of Sensation Affairs
That you, Dear Reader,
Conceive to be Other...

Between those two Forms
is a
Complex Dynamical Surface.

This Bounding Surface shall be Called...

Your Surface of Sensed Self.

Your Surface of Sensed Self, Dear Reader,

Being Complex,
Its Sensed Dynamics are Unfathomable.

Being Dynamical,
Its Sensed Complexity is Changing.

Your Surface of Sensed Self, Dear Reader,
is a
Complex Dynamical Sensed Surface.

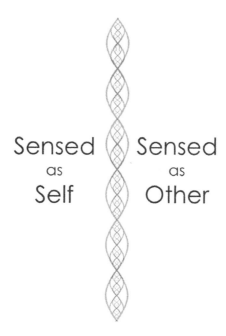

Sensed   Sensed
as   as
Self   Other

Two Forms of Behavior in Practice

Just as in the case of your Sensations,

likewise

Your Behaviors, Dear Reader,

are
Conceived as being

of
Two Primary Forms:

Self and Other.

On your Surface of Observation,

are

States of Behavior Affairs
Conceived to be Self

and

States of Behavior Affairs
Conceived to be Other.

Surface of Behaving Self

Between

Imagined and Observed
States of Behavior Affairs
That you, Dear Reader,
Conceive to be Self...

and

Imagined and Observed
States of Behavior Affairs
That you, Dear Reader,
Conceive to be Other...

Between those two Forms
is
A Complex Dynamical Surface.

This Bounding Surface shall be Called...

Your Surface of Behaving Self.

Your Surface of Behaving Self, Dear Reader,

Being Complex,
Its Behavior Dynamics are Unfathomable.

Being Dynamical,
Its Behavior Complexity is Changing.

Your Surface of Behaving Self, Dear Reader,
is
A Complex Dynamical Behavior Surface.

Behavior   Behavior
of   of
Self   Other

1st Practice of Domain Reduction

Prior to taking up the Work,

You, Dear Reader,

Conceive your Surface of Observation
to be of
Four Primary Domains:

Sensed Self
Sensed Other
Behaving Self
Behaving Other

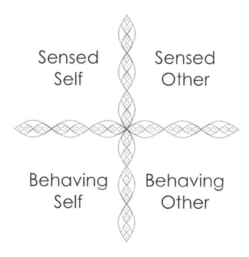

Sensed
Self

Sensed
Other

Behaving
Self

Behaving
Other

Sensing is Passive.

That part of Sensing
that is
Not Passive,

Shall be Called... Behaving.

Behaving is Active.

That part of Behaving
that is
Not Active,

Shall be Called... Sensing.

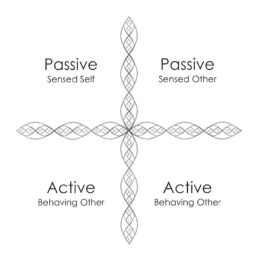

Passive
Sensed Self

Passive
Sensed Other

Active
Behaving Other

Active
Behaving Other

Having taken up the Work, Dear Reader,

You NOW Conceive your Surface of Observation
as
Only
Two Primary Domains:

Surface of Identity
&
Surface of Action

Having Reduced Dimensionality,
This shall be Called...

Dimensional Reduction.

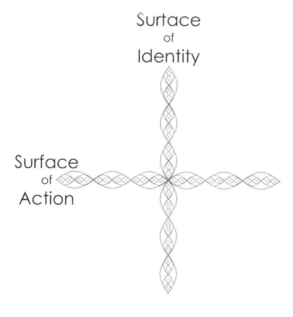

Surface
of
Identity

Surface
of
Action

2nd Practice of Domain Reduction

Behavior of Self...
Behavior of Other...
Sensation of Self...
Sensation of Other...

Reduced to two Boundaries...

Surface of Identity
&
Surface of Action...

Those two Boundaries
Comprise a Whole.

That Whole
Recognized as One

is

Fulfillment
of the
Second Practice of Domain Reduction
in your
Surface of Observation.

Sphere of Will Power in Practice

Your Sphere of Imagination, Dear Reader,
Is Said to be...

Your Sphere of Will Power.

Your Will cannot Act at your Origin;
Your Origin is Impossible.

Your Attention cannot be at your Origin;
Your Origin is Unknowable.

Your Will can Act at your Surface of Observation,
but is only a
Partial Power there...

For at your Surface of Observation,
Your Environment
is also a
Partial Power.

However...

In your Sphere of Imagination,

Your Will, Dear Reader,

Acts with Full Power.

Thus, your
Sphere of Imagination
Can be Called...

Your Sphere of Will Power.

Practicing Will to Life Flow

Your Life Flow, Dear Reader,

Radiates
as
Fluctuations in your Model...
Outward from your Origin

and

Reflects
as
Fluctuations in your Model...
Inward toward your Origin.

This
Radiation and Reflection

is Said to be...

Your Life Flow.

Futile Mass

Attracts your Attention Field,

Obstructs your Life Flow.

Futile Mass

also

Scatters your Attention Field,

Thus
Scattering
Your Life Flow.

Thus, your Practice, Dear Reader,
is to

By Will
Warp your Model

into
Life Flow...

by means of...

Preventing, Avoiding, and Melting
Futile Mass,

Which is Negative Practice...

and

Initiating, Attending, and Nurturing
Life Flow,

Which is Positive Practice.

Negative Practice is Brave.

Positive Practice is Wise.

Discernment of Futility & Power

The Practice

of

Will to Life Flow

in

Your Sphere of Imagination

Requires

a

Certain Understanding.

This Understanding

is

Both the Beginning and the End

of

All Practice.

This Understanding shall be Called...

Discernment of Futility and Power.

The Student Wills to Life Flow

by
Discerning

That which is Futile
and
That which is Powerful.

By
Restoring Life Flow,

The Student
is
Made Able to Discern

That which is Futile
and
That which is Powerful.

Discernment Restores Life Flow
and
Life Flow makes Discernment Possible.

The Snake Eats Its Tail.

Understanding Gives
Birth to Life.

Life Gives
Birth to Understanding

Will.

Infinite Nesting of Domains

Each Domain of your Model, Dear Reader,

is

an
Infinite Nesting...
within
Infinite Nesting...
within
Infinite Nesting...
w i t h i n
I n f i n i t e   N e s t i n g ...

of

Infinite Nested Nests

of

Infinite Subdomains

Forever and so on.

Careless Student Lost in Nests

A Careless Student

was
Once Lost in Nests.

Thus...

A Simple Warning...

Losing One Self in Nests...

Such is Not the Work.

Zero Rule of Thumb

Infinite are the Paths,
but
One is the Work.

How might a Student
Recognize the Work?

As you Progress with the Work, Dear Reader,

Spaces Reduce to Boundary Surfaces
and
Boundary Surfaces Reduce to One.

Such is the Work.

Understanding this, Dear Reader,

You are Doing the Work.

The Unity of the Poles
is
The Very Difference of the Poles.

The Difference of the Poles
is
The Very Unity of the Poles.

Understanding this, Dear Reader,
You are Doing the Work.

Zero Master

The Master once Said...

One is Never One.

The Student Responded...

Many is Never Many.

For Brevity...

The Master Simply Says...

Zero

.

Again... The Warning

You, Dear Reader,

Eat the very Meal you Prepare.

The Universe, Dear Reader,

Reflects Exactly You.

As you do unto Others,

Likewise is done to you.

Reflecting Forms,

Returning You to You,

Are as you have Willed,

Although Transformed.

Each Student Does Find...

That

Will to Both

Give and Receive

Life...

Will to Restore

Life Flow...

is in
ItSelf

Beauty...

Love...

Truth

.

As
You,

with
Genuine Understanding,

BOTH

Possess and Use
the
Antidote...

You Are NOW
A Keeper of the Real Wooden Stake.

.

You Are
as
You Will
as
You Are
as
You Will
as
You Are
as
You Will
as
You Are
as
You Will
as

.

No More Accident

Before Genuinely Understanding the Work...

You, Dear Reader, could be Called...

An Accidental Vampire.

Not Genuinely Understanding,

You Willed Futilely...

You Blocked the Flow of Attention...
You Willed Life Drains.

By Insinuating and Blocking,
You Willed Life Drain in your Neighbors.

By Suspicion and Blocking,
You Willed Life Drain in yourself.

Expressing

The Absence of Genuine Understanding,

with

Combinations
of
Hinting and Blocking...

You, Dear Reader,

Vampired in Every Domain...

ACCIDENTALLY.

NOW

Genuinely Understanding the Work,

No More Accident.

NOW, Dear Reader,

To Begin Again...

Such is the Work.

Life Inevitable

With or without you, Dear Reader,

Life goes on.

Shall you take up the Work Anew?

Shall you Will Attention to Life Flow?

Shall you, ever more, Cease to Block?

Shall you Warp your Model

such that

Suspicions Manifest Living
and
Your Insinuations Inspire Life Flow?

You, Dear Reader, Will.

Afterword

A Note on Compassion

Prior to Genuinely Understanding the Work...

Each of us, without exception, is an Accidental Vampire.

Just as a young child is
Not to be judged, blamed, or criticized
For Not yet Knowing what they have Not yet Learned,

likewise...

No Accidental Vampire is to be judged, blamed, or criticized
For Not yet Knowing what they have Not yet Learned.

You and I, Dear Reader, have both been Accidental
Vampires,
And so also have been our Neighbors.
Thus...

Judge Not
is ever
Written in the Hearts of the Wise.

As for those few...

For whom Vampirism is no longer Accidental...

Their Reflection shall ever be their own Reward.

We need Not assist...

As the Universe is ever Its Own Perfect Mirror.

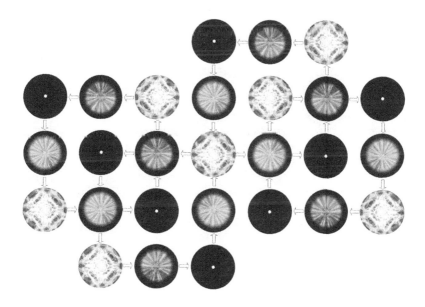

Thus, Dear Reader... Practice Compassion,

For likewise...

Your Reward is ever Your Own Reflection.

Thanks

First and foremost... I THANK my Parents and Grandparents...
For Guiding me, from the beginning, into a Life of LOVE.
There is surely no greater Gift than LOVE in Life.

Second... I THANK Master Kwan, who's daily reminders...

Where Attention goes, Life Flows...

Turned my Attention toward Attention Itself.

Third... I THANK my Dear Friends,
Who have patiently Listened and Reflected
My deepest considerations... all along the Way.
It is by your Kind and Generous Reflecting Ears that any
Clarity has been achieved in these Subtle Domains.

Last, but most assuredly Not least...
I THANK Sweet LOVE Sunshine,
Who has Walked with me so Kindly...
Who has held my Hand and Heard my Thoughts...
Who has Inspired...
And countless other LOVING Things...
Far beyond words.
Your Questions inspired this very Work and
Your Sweet LOVE makes it Possible.

Accidental Vampires
&
The Real Wooden Stake

Book 1: Initiation

Thomas Orr Anderson

Made in the USA
Monee, IL
30 January 2021

59183879R00125